FINISHING LINE PRESS

www.finishinglinepress.com

Circle the Bones
with Shining

poems by

Andréana Elise

Finishing Line Press
Georgetown, Kentucky

Circle the Bones
with Shining

ACKNOWLEDGMENTS

Thy name is my healing, prayer quoted in "A lamp is lit" is by Baha'u'llah:
https://www.bahaiprayers.org/healing2.htm

Publisher: Leah Huete de Maines
Editor: Christen Kincaid
Cover Art: © Beth Yazhari, *Radiant Orb*
Author Photo: Nadji Hedjazi
Cover Design: Elizabeth Maines McCleavy

Order online: www.finishinglinepress.com
also available on amazon.com

Author inquiries and mail orders:
Finishing Line Press
P. O. Box 1626
Georgetown, Kentucky 40324
U. S. A.

Table of Contents

Night

Morning

for Jackie,
who loved

and all women,
who heal

Someone sang for me and no one else could hear it.

Joy Harjo

Night

Can you see them?

Can you see them?

They are gathering—
the shining women,
with flowing hips and rainbow skin,
water jugs balanced
on their skulls.

They carry
grass baskets of cassava bread
and mangrove crabs caught
by hand in the thick heat,
thighs dark
with mud.

They are coming
to feed and swaddle us,
to free the oppressed
and bind us to what we flee
and must come home to,
immediately.

Look at the bruises on their arms,
the risen scars on their backs,
the silent wounds in their minds,
and their own bright bodies
condemned to dust—
rising again and again
in rapture.

Will you join them?

The shining women who circle the earth,
alive with spirit, at play with the work
we are brought here to do.

Their hidden crowns make flower
white roses from dead thorns,
and their kohl-rimmed eyes
are black as the night that births

light upon light
into our world.

Will you join them at the feast
they've spread,
under the olive and fig trees?

They've come with pomegranate seeds
and wheat for planting.
They've charred peppers and crushed
maize for stew.

They've drawn water from the river,
which is sweet again,
and touched a drop to our foreheads
so we can think clearly
and eat well

and dance—with naked feet
and hair flying—
long into the night.

When she was young

When she was young

my mother danced
with the crane-women of the south.

She was on an island at the bottom of the world.
She was praying and praying and the answer
led her deeper into the outback.

One night, she was invited to a corroboree.
Men lit a fire and grandmothers sat
on aluminum stools and watched.

The women began a brolga dance.

Brolga birds are known
for their exquisite courtship dances.
Long legs, balletic.

They asked my mother to join
and she did.

At the end, the women's arms
came up and down. Up and down.

Like wings coming down
onto this sea of water…

You tell me this story

You tell me this story
in your big white bed
before choosing to go to hospice.

When the ambulance arrives,
the drivers—both women with warm,
caramel eyes—carry you downstairs

laughing and joking, while
I remain, at the foot of your bed,
shrouded in silence.

The ceremony is over—
or is it just beginning? I cannot sing
or dance and the drums are slowing.

Who will help me? How will I pack
your things and remake the bed,
indented and still warm?

Shimmering through white
gauze curtains, the April night hides
ancestors in rank upon shining rank.

The women's wings have flown
from your youth
into this dream I am living,

carrying me to the door
of splendor,
waiting for my feet to take me in.

A lamp is lit

A lamp is lit beside the bed.
My mother is asleep, her breathing labored.
Sitting down, I take her hand.

Touching my forehead to our fingers,
I hum out of tune
the same words you once
prayed over me—

> *thy name is my healing*
> *and remembrance*
> *my remedy*

your arm across my shoulders,
resting together, in one big chair
in the sunshine.

This afternoon, you laughed

This afternoon, you laughed and prayed
with all the friends who came to say goodbye.

You listened with one hand pressed to heart,
eyebrows together, dark eyes closed, enrapt.
Now, you are resting, you are close.

Your moonshine skin is smooth, not gaunt.
Long brown hair has dissolved into silver down.
Nails once gnawed are ridged now, hands calm.

The catheter has only an inch or so of dark urine.
The nurse told us this would happen, as your body shuts down,
taking in less fluid, no food.

Yet somehow you radiate heat, filling the air with dense light.
The light curls in rainbow serpents from you into us.

The air is fire and it is hard to breathe.

When the last

When the last few visitors arrive, I want them to leave.
I want you to myself.
Grateful they see your beauty,
I am jealous of your attention.
You see me, seated alone by the window,
apart from the circle surrounding you.
You peek around the body of a friend,

and wink at me.

I've been waiting

I've been waiting for you,
I'm so happy you're here.

you say.

You almost had

You almost had a sister,
did you know that?

You almost had a sister
with blue-black skin
and hair that curled
like bushfire smoke.

I was living in Northern Australia,
barely twenty-six, sewing my own clothes,
lotus flowers behind my ear.

Her uncles and aunties
wanted a better life for her.
And I was a teacher, single,
American.

They wanted their child to fly
across the ocean on silver wings,
to the golden streets
they saw on TV.

But too many children had been stolen,
losing their language, their faces,
their breath.

Would adoption be any different?

I held Anita close
and her hair smelled like sea salt.
How could I strip that salt
from her hair?

When I painted her face
ceremonial white,
the ochre stained my hands.

How could I wash
the colors from her skin?

In town, we went to a restaurant
to eat fish, but the angry white
eyes turned my stomach.

How could I make those eyes
her daily life?

I left Anita on the island in 1978
and haven't been back since.

I am your only

I am your only child,
my father's fifth.

At twenty-three, I am wise
and foolish enough

to think you will live
if I bring ice cream on a wicker tray.

If I wash your hair and trim your nails.

If I forget myself
in words and record your life story,

legs curled beneath me
and tired. My God, so tired.

You tell me to eat, to rest.
Instead, I vacuum the floor and wipe

the wooden table by your bed,
where the giver of life

has scattered dust—soft and white—
for me to follow.

Hours pass, or days

Hours pass, or days.

I take a cotton cloth
from the bedside table,

walk to the sink by the door,
and run the tap until it's warm.

Wring out the cloth,
wipe your forehead and cheeks,
the corners of your mouth and eyes.

With a pink sponge on a stick
I moisten your tongue,
cool your ears with my cold hands.

Lying on your back in bed,
the flame of your body is dim,
but the light in your face is clear

and shining.

These last months

These last months, more than anything,
I want to go home, to the island.

To see the children, wiry limbed
and crackling with life,

just like their grandmas.

Eileen, in her seventies,
jumped from the back of a moving truck

and caught a goanna with her bare hands.

She threw the six foot lizard
to the ground and broke its neck,

then draped the body over her shoulders
and walked back to us, smiling.

She left bushmeat in tin cans
on my doorstep,

and when I joked *What about mangrove worms?*
she laughed and said I wouldn't enjoy

wriggling spaghetti. But I learned to eat
turtle and crab, fried breadfruit

and the rare imported orange.

At dusk, my hair dried to copper wire
by the sun, I knelt by offerings too ripe

for eating, in the dirt under sacred pukumani—
carved spirits of the dead.

Here, a few feet from the ocean,
insects and ghosts gather and tease the living,

tasting my sweetness
in the fading red light.

We used to sit

We used to sit together and pray.
As a child, it was when I felt closest to you.

You threw back your head and called loudly to God.
A blue-black shawl kept your body from flying away.

You rose and sank in rhythm to the recitation,
the lines of your face mapping a strong and lovely light.

I watched and bowed down too,
until my forehead warmed the backs of my hands.

Did I ever tell you what I heard, what I saw
in those bright places behind the backs of my hands?

Is it too late to tell you now?

In the garden

In the garden behind my eyes
you stand, knee-deep in mud,

digging up red clay,
laying down rich, black soil.

I wait in the doorway, wanting
you to come inside, unable
to say why.

Why is it so hard to speak
the words, *I'm lonely?*

Instead, I call from the doorway,
Mom come inside, dinner's ready.

You turn to me, then turn away,
garden hose in hand,

cotton pajamas sprigged
with pink flowers, legs rolled up,
feet bare.

Some nights, I walked

Some nights, I walked barefoot
by the ocean, so alone

I thought my blood
would combust.

The sky churned with bright foam—
stars like stones

in the fields my mother worked
as a girl, picking rocks white
as bone

in the wake of glaciers.
Stone by stone, she prepared the land
for planting.

My letters home are poor
attempts to share this new world

that has swallowed me whole,
cleaned me out and filled me with—

You!

A shout for joy

big

and beautiful

as this holy night—

sea of stars and milk white moon—

waves of light,

washing through me.

Stripped bare

Stripped bare in this nowhere place
between one grief and the next
I go to your garden, seeking

you, and the one within you too.
I cut white roses from the branch,
petals damp with drops of rain

so soft against the brightness
of my skin. I wrap their stems
in tin foil to take with me,

the next time I visit you.
The day we learned the illness
had come back, my childhood

fear was justified. How many nights
I worried you would die,
guarding the breath that rose and fell

in your stomach, even as my own breath
grew small and tight, a fist of light
so dense, it knocked the wind from my lungs

and wrestled the angel from my bones,
cutting her hair and denying
her hunger.

Have you ever felt

Have you ever felt God's fist?
The knuckles are worn as hillsides in Haifa,
where I lived as a girl, in the crook of the sea.
Like my mother and great-grandmother,
I too crossed oceans, not out of choice
but compulsion. This is the truth:
I was hungry for many years. Spirit took
my animal body in her arms and shook it,
clogging my eyes and nostrils with so much dust
I lost my way.
In the desert, you eat what you can find.
Sorrow is a bitter root,
and I ate it, night after night. What does
a girl of fifteen have to grieve?
Just look around. My blood dried up,
and my mother feared, and my father
couldn't understand though he tried.
This is the lie: Life is suffering.
It is also true, until you kneel in God's fist,
covered in oleander and wild thyme,
when the sea is dark with night,
and you beg those knotted fingers to open—
and, years and years later,
they do.

First though

First though, the Fist closes tight,
so tight you can't breathe or speak,
so tight your skin blisters in the heat
of closeness to some other realm of being.

The kingdom long promised is far, far away.
Instead, here is the pit—
a fist of stone with you in its grip.
Pressing soft cheeks against
this unrelenting rock

you stay up, night after night,
listening to the wind and waiting,
waiting for the chink of light
that signals day.

I cannot see

I cannot see how light I am—
my see-through skin,
veins blossoming blue and green
through thin arms,
my skull beneath flesh
tender as a knife
lifting, lifting
the meat from the bone.

My hips and shoulder blades
are sharp as my father's intake of breath—
as he looks at me, then looks away,
as I change into a thin cotton robe
open at the back—
revealing my spinal cord,
the fine clawmarks
of my ribs.

My mother is bereft.
Wearing horn earrings and an onyx ring,
she confronts the disease in me:

> *If you do not eat this food,*
> *you will not come home.*
> *I will not accept your denial*
> *one more time.*

And I weep as I eat
choking down the breadcrumbs,
my fragmented heart
unholy on my tongue.

Who nurses us

Who nurses us through the night?
Who lifts us
wailing
in the mermaid-tailed
darkness, who prays
over us, rocking,
in the watery
predawn light?

After starvation
and the hospital,
they send me home
with a tube down my nose
for night feedings.
But the voices in my head
are too loud to ignore—
hijacking control—
offering salvation
by trading bread and butter
for a belt of thorns.

Carefully,
I unhook the feeding tube,
filling a silver basin
with rivers of milk and honey
that should be flowing
into my bloodstream.

Softly,
I pour out the remedy,
and return to bed,
concealing my crime as best I can.
But the ones who watch over me
find out,
and I sleep with my mother
that night,
and many nights to come,

so she can guard
the machine that feeds me,
keeping me alive.

God knows
if you slept at all,
waiting—
not for my cry—
but for the silence
of my body
under the blanket—
your child stolen away
by this burning
in my brain.

This prayer is

This prayer is
for my daughter.

I see you

balanced in body soul spirit
robust, joyful

your true and real self.

You will discover
the truth within you

Be

completely and utterly
healed.

All assistance will be granted.

You can't keep on

You can't keep on like this,

you tell me in early spring
before going to hospice.

I don't know how you're still standing,
sitting with me here today.

It is time now, to take care of yourself.

But my desire to be in this world
is guttering fast.

And without you,
why mend the lamp?

Why last?

One night, you

One night, you give me a piece of driftwood
inlaid with amber, turquoise.

It's carved with the words
the elders gave you, long ago:

> *In the dreamtime,*
> *I will sing you*
> *to me.*

How can a slender branch washed ashore
god knows where

singe me with such wonder,
wound me with such love?

There is a fire in the holy tree, Mother,
and you gave me a twig—

to kindle my darkness
and not be consumed.

Tonight, I bring

Tonight, I bring food
to the hospice—

fruit and yogurt, nothing much.
I eat, even though you can't.

How can I?

How can I not
blame myself?

I asked your forgiveness
in your big white bed

and one look washed away
all guilt and shame.

Promises are simple,
and I promise to live.

The flyer read

The flyer read
"Victoria Teacher Exchange Program."

It was stuck to a bulletin board
at the UND student union
and I grabbed it and flew—

away from my family, from Dakota,
those flat golden fields
dipped in so much blood,
and lonelier than hell.

But when I arrived in Perth,
10,224 miles later,
the same blood was on my hands,
in the streets,
the same burning in my skin—

hurled into a world
where skin and sex,
status and name—
and god knows even weight—
brand some as human and others

untouchable
woman
slave.

The children in my classroom—
mostly migrants and a few silent
Aboriginal girls and boys—

wrote new laws and taught me to trust
the message coming strong and sweet:

Return to those flat red innerlands.
We're waiting for you there.

In preparation for the journey,
I ate and emptied myself,
begged for wisdom,
praying hard.

So when my forehead touched the ground—
I knew.

The crowds behind my eyelids
shouted for mercy
then grew silent.

Explosions
of praise drowned out my lamenting.

I was home.

Reunited with this
holy and unbinding
protecting and unfolding
holding and releasing
love in us.

The ceiling fan purred.

Heat curled from my body into angelic hosts
on my right, on my left,
above my head, in the ground deep within—

and I saw

protestors kneeling on the bridge between worlds,
lifting dark fingers to loosen
the noose.

My mother rose from the ranks and came toward me.
She was black
and her bones glowed, visible, through her skin.

You are just as much my own
as the rest, she said.

You are no outcast, no orphan,
no reject from God's pottery wheel.

At the table of all beings,
there is a seat just for you.

I shuddered then, all the pent up
grief and rage passing through me in sobs and gasps

as I grasped her hand and she
handed me—

my soul—
such a small tender thing,

so vast and compactly made,
perfect as I can never be.

Detonating serenity
from its bottomless depths—

I swallowed it whole—
blue fields of darkness and mansions of
great light—

then lifted my head,
and opened my eyes.

The night is gold

The night is gold and emerald black.

A woman chants in Arabic.
Her voice is a beam of light…

wheeling, calling me
through the trees.
Am I sleeping?
No, last night I stayed here, awake,
unfearing, keeping watch.

This morning, I drove home,
covered myself in white blankets
and dreamed…
running barefoot through dark
streets, past sleeping houses.
A woman sings, bodiless, in the trees.

How did I get here?
My hair is wet from a shower
I can't remember taking…

fireflies trail me—
ranks of angels?

Who is with me?
I am not alone, but all is shadowed
in a dark and absolving gold.

Everything is still

Everything is still
until
you sweep your arm
from under the covers—

calling me.

Friends leave

Friends leave.
Dad and I drive
home

guided
by a full moon haloed
      in blackness.

Morning

The morgue is

The morgue is hard and white.
Light infiltrates even the dark sides of objects.

We have stepped into the center of revelation—
all mysteries are laid bare.

The body is

The body is on a table in the middle of the room.

Your body is on a table
        and seven women surround it.

The room is

The room is white,
and light penetrates even the dark interiors of objects.
I am one of the women surrounding the body.
I am—and I am not.
For it is hard to see,
hard to know if I really am here—or not.
One of the women begins to chant in Arabic.
I am holding a small phial of attar from Damascus.
Soap is passed from hand to hand.
Water spurts from a tap at the feet of the corpse.
We use our hands and white cloths to bathe you.
The prayers continue. Singing.
One voice or many, I cannot tell.
My eyes are closed.
They are open.
How am I here? How am I still standing?
The singing has become my legs.
My body has become the singing.
Am I singing? No, I am silent.
I am the black stone
around which the singing turns, and multiplies—
a river stone, washed by women's voices.
They hold me up,
bright slip of a girl,
washing the body of my mother.

This body

This body.
This house of flesh covering bone.
Riven by one cell on fire,
red buds of cancer eating the skin beneath the breast.
I wash these too, they are part of the structure now.
I wash the entrances, the orifices,
the gates through which the world goes and comes.
I wash
your ears
your eyes
your lips
your cheeks
your shoulders
your breasts
your belly
your thighs
your shins
your slender ankles
your high-arched feet.
I kiss your forehead,
your small mouth,
once, twice. I lose count.
The flesh of the body is already mottled—
bruises of a world desperate to hold onto this creation,
already beyond its grasp.

You slip from us

You slip from us, surround us,
embrace and negate us.
The body is not my mother.
Whatever you are and are-not
leaps and cartwheels around us,
pulsing through the cold, white room
like blood through and around
my own neglected bones.

This room

This room is a mirror
and I am reflected in the wings
of your body, closed and hard,
but still full of shining.
I am reflected in the secret face, the ancient hands—
the oldest hands in the world—
and the young, the ever-young
hips
and thighs
and ankles.

The phial

The phial has marked my clenched palm.
I pull out the stopper.
The room is filled with the scent of rose—
with the crushed essence
of a thousand thousand thorny heads.
Five pieces of silk were sewn into one long sheet.
Seven women wrap one woman
in the white clothes of a pilgrim.

Who is singing?

Who is singing?
I am.
Am I?
I am.
Are you sure?
I am.
How do you know?
The sound of the wind in the trees
is now my breath,
which is the sound of the waving ocean,
which is my own blood
wounding my ears
with its own sweet rushing.
I am.
I am.
I am this sweet rushing.

Your body is

Your body is lifted up.
Who conducts this lifting and falling
into the hand-carved, oak-wood vessel?

I slip two rings onto your fingers.
One holds a prayer, and the other—
slim beaten band—
is a promise, just between us.

The face of the queen

The face of the queen in the coffin
is not the face of the body before it was washed.

The reflection in your face is greater now
than the combined illumination

of seven women washing a corpse and singing—
which is the closest I've ever come to the sun.

I cannot keep my eyes open.
But it is not dark when I close them.

For the first time, my own body—
my own dark interior—
is luminous.

By washing your body

By washing your body and adorning it,
my own body is washed and adorned.
I can no longer hate
my hands,
old like yours, and beautiful.
I can no longer hate
my body—
this gentle motion of washing and adorning,
wrapping and perfuming,
singing and releasing.

The layers of disease and suffering
are quietly sloughed away,
softly lapped away from us both,
by water and song and the scent of rose.
I am alone.
Where have the others gone?
They are in a cold, white room.
So where are you?
Where am I?

The bones of my body

The bones of my body have opened—
white roses in the sun.

And my blood
my skin
my sinew

all my organs are chanting,
ululating
in my native tongue.

In a white room

In a white room,
on the outskirts of a large city,
my mother is prepared for burial.

We wash you,
wrap you, and pray
for your safe keeping.

Before leaving,
I give each woman a river
stone from Haiti,
where an earthquake
has killed thousands.
And to each, a piece of dark
chocolate, for sweetness
and strength.

They enfold me in their bodies,
these sisters,
breathing softly.

Holy Mother, please
be with me
now.

Lift your head

Lift your head,
spread your wings,
dig your heels into the red earth.

Dust rises,
bright winds
twist around our bodies

as we whirl and jump
stomp and sway
leap and fly

flame shooting off the blades of our bones
the sheath of our flesh

as we bow deep
splay our feet
reach high

and ride the Spirit as she swoops
low and gold
over the homeland of our people.

This is the dance
of the crane-women
of the south

This is the dance
we did not know
we knew

so well, so deep
inside the marrow
of our soul.

We scoop and slide
dip and squat

kneel and press

our breasts,
our bellies, our thighs
into the red earth.

Blue ash
sighs and smears our skin
the color of creation

and we arch our necks
raise our throats, open our wings
and step

into air upheld
by drums, by trumpets

by men's beating palms
and roaring breath.

The crane-women
painted white
flap and enfold us—

broad-hipped, long-legged
the red spot on their heads
marking the place

where each day they enter
and carry back to us
a drop of the rising sun.

We circle our wrists
sweep our arms
plant our feet

and fill our lungs with night
made red and bright

by god's fire, men's tools
and women's song.

Ommmmmm.
Ommmmmm.

The digeridoo calls

and you respond
with a whisper

in the back of your throat

that no one hears
but me

a long time later
and many lives away—

dreaming us, dancing

with the crane-women
of the south

heads lifted, hips opens,
thighs strong,

hair flying

cheeks red as sunrise
faces shining with waters

feet barely touching
the burning earth.

I will sing

I will sing you to me,
you say, before you die.

It was night then,
and we were all gathered.

A note on the title:

In a little book my mother, Jacqueline, gave me,
she underlined this poem by Stephen Spender—

"Bright clasp of her whole hand around my finger,
my daughter, as we walk together now.
<u>*All my life I'll feel a ring invisibly*</u>
<u>*Circle this bone with shining*</u> *: when she is grown*
Far from today as her eyes are far already."

Gratitudes

This book was midwifed by many shining people, a few of whom I want to thank by name:

Tim Rogers, healer and kindred spirit, who loved and listened me back into being.

Janet Harrison, love-giver, lightworker and poet, who taught me gentleness and believed I could write myself well.

Judith Benkendorf, who keeps the spirit of Mom's garden alive in Santa Fe, NM, where Mrs. Buddha (aka Kwan Yen, the Goddess of Compassion) prays for us all, under the turquoise skies.

Susan Christianson, heart-mother and wisdom-walker, who carried the Crane Dance poem back to Australia, where Mom found her Baha'i Faith.

Kris Whorton, teacher, strengthener and friend, who was the first person to read the full manuscript and encouraged me to dig deep. Then deeper.

Sandra Hutchison, nourisher and soul-kin, who found me online, reached out, and discovered…an endless chorus of *selahs.* Thank you for also connecting me with Beth Yazhari, whose "Radiant Orb," graces the cover.

Ilona Surgaile, whose clear eyes Saw my book in action, while we served together, at the Baha'i Temple in Wilmette.

Helen Butler, inspirer and one of my tribe, for sheer delight and joy in the process!

Elisa Negroni, illuminator, neighbor, sister-friend, who helped me unravel the songlines within.

Barbara Miller and Vahid Alavian, who believed in me, adopted me, and gave me refuge.

Jacoba and Ravosh Samari, who welcomed me in, and provided safe haven as I birthed this book.

To my soul-sisters and brothers: You know who you are. I thank Creator each and every day for your presence, which has the power to transform "a drop of water into rivers and seas and an atom into lights and suns."

To the women who circled our family during and after Mom's passing: You gave us life.

Susan Troxel, who came weekly to sit with Mom, and to listen and love us.

Lida Taghinia, who was there when Mom passed, and gave me the gift of her own life story.

The Jarrah sisters: Hala, Huda, Zenouba, and Maha. Auntie Hala's Arabic chanting surrounded Mom as she left this world, and the rest of us, as we washed her body.

Lisa Glines, who captured precious last moments on film.

Angel, a real-life soul conductor, who assisted us in washing Mom's body.

Sesi, who drove the ambulance, taking Mom to hospice, and came back to visit, with flowers.

To my ancestors, known and unknown: thank you for this body. My body. My life.

To You—yes, You, reading this—thank you, beyond words.

Dad: There are no words. Except one. Liminal. I'll meet you there.

And last, because I want your name to live in every heart: Jacqueline Tahirih, also called Miridinga by the Tiwi People.

Mom: I'm in a house full of love and good food, near the ocean. There's garlic frying, cool winds blowing, and I'm keeping my promise. L'chaim.

Andréana Elise is a poet, essayist, educator, and community grower. Traveling between countries and cultures, she works to end cycles of violence, heal trauma, and embody justice through freeing the voice. She teaches creative writing in jails and recovery programs, and collaborates with artists and activists of all backgrounds, creating spaces of refuge for the human spirit: www.andreana-elise.com

www.ingramcontent.com/pod-product-compliance
Lightning Source LLC
Chambersburg PA
CBHW021201090426
42740CB00008B/1184